Bella and me

Bella and me

Life in the service of a cat

Herblock

Bonus Books, Inc., Chicago

99 98 97 96 95   5 4 3 2 1

Library of Congress Cataloging-in-Publication Data

Block, Herbert, 1909–
    Bella and me: life in the service of a cat/Herblock.
        p. cm.
    ISBN 1-56625-052-8 (hardcover)
    1. Cats—Washington (D.C.)—Biography.   2. Block, Herbert,
1909–   I. Title.
SF445.5.B59   1995   95-42706
818'.5403—dc20

Bonus Books, Inc.
160 East Illinois Street
Chicago, Illinois 60611

Composition by Point West, Inc.
Printed in the United States of America

Also by Herbert Block

Herblock: A Cartoonist's Life
Herblock at Large
Herblock Through the Looking Glass
Herblock on All Fronts
Herblock Special Report
Herblock's State of the Union
The Herblock Gallery
Straight Herblock
Herblock's Special for Today
Herblock's Here and Now
The Herblock Book

I found her under a bush.

More accurately, I first *saw* her under a bush. It was in the back yard next to the steps and porch that led to my first-floor apartment. She was a brand new kitten looking up at the world with big wondering eyes. She was mostly black, with white cheeks, white paws and a little black spot on her mouth that gave her the appearance of constantly saying, "Oh!"

Her mother was an alley cat who trusted nobody. Mama cat marched back and forth in front of her offspring and did everything but handstands to divert my attention from baby cat. She had also cleverly chosen to give birth not only behind a bush, but in front of a loose board in the back yard fence. So when her distractions failed and I came too close, she could shift to Plan B: Move kitten through fence into other yard.

There may have been more kittens on one side of the fence or the other. But this was the fluffy little thing that fascinated me, and I began wooing.

I put out little saucers of milk for her. While mama cat watched and paced around anxiously, I placed food and drink closer to the steps and then on the steps themselves, beginning with the bottom one. Day by day and step by step, I carried on what the neighbors recognized as a shameless courtship. Eventually she was enticed to the porch and then to the open door of my apartment, but not without chaperoning by her mother who kept a careful distance behind.

From the beginning the kitten's name was Bella. It seemed to fit, and besides I had once bet on a horse named Bell The Cat. The watchful mother, I decided, was the Madame—or Moddom.

Moddom was tough but not entirely wild. When I finally got Bella to come into the house for occasional meals, Moddom recognized the realities and we discussed the situation. I explained that I could give Bella a happy home and keep her well-fed and that she could still go outdoors. Moddom was particularly interested in seeing that her daughter would continue to have access to the yard, that she—Moddom—wary though she was, would have full visitation rights, and that her daughter would be brought up as a bona fide authentic independent cat. She would be her mother's daughter, despite the relatively effete enclosed quarters that I could provide. Neither of us mentioned it, but, of course, Moddom was free to pursue all her outside activities unencumbered. There was nothing in her terms that I couldn't agree to; and I assured her that she, Moddom, could think of my apartment as a home of her own. This part she did not accept or decline.

The upshot was that Bella came to live with me; and Moddom later came to visit.

Bella got used to the house, which she explored thoroughly. There were stacks of papers to hide behind and climb over. She would pop up unexpectedly almost anywhere. Whenever I pulled out a partially open file drawer I might find that Bella had filed herself in it.

She also turned up in my shoes, in closets and any shelves, cabinets, drawers or boxes she could get into. It didn't take her long to learn things like How To Interfere With His Work, which included walking across a moving typewriter carriage; and the psychic phenomenon of How To Outsit Him. This meant not only using my favorite chair, but sensing when I was *thinking* of sitting in it, so that she could get there first.

During her kittenhood, Bella was quite the ingenue, and it didn't take much to surprise her. When I was barefoot, she would examine my feet with wonder. And when I suddenly turned up my toes, she flew a couple of inches straight up in the air. Not backward or forward or from a crouching position—straight up.

Of course, she engaged in furniture-prowling, which included walking along the narrow back of a sofa that stood against a long library table. Once, while a friend and I were sitting on the couch, Bella was demonstrating some impressive imaginary tightrope walking when her foot slipped and her leg dropped between sofa and table. She looked dismayed and embarrassed. My companion, a woman with a good understanding of cats, immediately said that we must not laugh. For a young cat to lose its balance like that could be traumatic, practically bringing into question its entire cathood.

"THAT'S MY TAIL"

Sometimes, as she made her way along the couch ledge, I would gently take Bella's tail in my fingers. At this she would turn disapprovingly and say, "That's my *tail*." And gathering herself with pride, she would walk on, saying, "I have my dignity."

"I HAVE MY DIGNITY"

Bella was free to go out to the porch and yard, where she could visit her mother when Moddom was in residence there. She also took to a life of adventure, prowling through weeds and making like the Big Cats Of Africa. She might have been pretending she was stalking something, although this was evidently beyond her.

On one of her expeditions, she was padding along the walkway next to the house when a little mouse appeared. It was hard to tell which was more surprised, Bella or the mouse. They looked at each other in brief astonishment. Then Bella watched the mouse run off— and after a pause, hopped after it. The mouse quickly disappeared into a drain pipe, which Bella inspected with simple curiosity. I think she felt she had found and lost a little playmate. She was too young and inexperienced to be the mighty hunter Moddom was. But she managed to find excitement anyhow.

There was, for example, The Encounter With The Kleenex Box. While nosing around a table to see what she could discover, she came upon the box topped with its plume of white Kleenex. She put her paws up on the box and pushed her nose against the tissue, which bent. She made a tentative pass at it, and it moved. She then went at the tissue more vigorously, taking swipes with her paw and tugging with her mouth until she finally pulled it completely out of the box. But to her amazement another tissue now occupied the same place atop the box. She knew a challenge when she saw it and lost no time in going on the offensive. No sooner had she yanked out the second tissue than another appeared.

She didn't know what variant of mythological creature she might be up against, but after only a moment's bewilderment, she resumed the attack with quickened pace. Working faster, she tore into the tissues, pulling out one after another until table and floor were littered with them. I didn't want to deprive her of total victory, but finally decided to put the box away before I had wall-to-wall Kleenex carpeting. She didn't seem to mind. She surveyed all the soft white objects she had vanquished, poked and stomped on a few of them, and seemed pleased with herself. She might even have felt that Moddom would be proud be of her.

Bella always seemed to know when Moddom was on the porch. She would go bounding to the door and look up expectantly at me. One night I opened the door for her, and sure enough Moddom was waiting. I could see by the dim porch light that mother had brought something to show daughter. It was the head of a rat. Bella looked at it and said, "Oh." When I realized what it was, I kicked it under the porch railing and into the yard below. Moddom watched it go by and instantly looked up in amazement and outrage. "What have you done?" she demanded. "Why did you do that?" I didn't know what to tell her.

True, I had agreed that Bella was to be brought up as a complete certified self-contained cat with links to mama and the outside world. And I knew that Moddom was an excellent ratter. It just hadn't occurred to me that she would be bringing a rat's head to my door. I left Bella and Moddom outside and closed the door. If Moddom took Bella downstairs, retrieved the treasure and gave Bella instructions in ratting, that was up to her. I thought it was a little early for Bella to learn ratting—and didn't care if she ever took it up. When she returned, I was rather relieved that she showed no signs of being interested in anything but her usual dinner fare and games of hide and seek.

In time Moddom cautiously accepted my invitation to come in. She would come to the door to see Bella and later would guardedly enter to have dinner with her offspring while keeping an eye on me and making sure the door remained open. When I first tried easing the door shut, she went into a kind of W.C. Fields routine, crying, "Look out, I think he's going to pull a knife. He's out to get us," and darted out the door. Eventually she was willing to stay inside, even with the door closed, and—particularly as the weather grew colder—she decided to sleep over, spending the night. She also gave Bella tail training, sitting in a chair and switching her tail while Bella tried to grab it.

But the call of the outdoors was too strong for Moddom to remain a permanent houseguest. One morning I got up to find her missing. Bella and I did a survey of the apartment with no result. Moddom had found a window facing the yard, open just wide enough for her to scrunch through, leap out and resume her neighborhood prowling and hunting. But the yard remained her home base and special domain.

Another morning I got up at daybreak with full intention of returning directly from bathroom to bed, when I looked out the window and saw Moddom crouching on the ground and looking up at a small grape arbor that formed a nook next to the fence. Atop the arbor sat another cat. It looked ahead at nothing in particular. It just sat there. Moddom never took her eyes off the intruder. Slowly, belly close to the ground, Moddom took a careful step forward and stopped. Then after awhile, eyes still fastened on the other cat, another slow step forward and another stop. With one slow silent step at a time, she approached the trellis. While the Moddom's eyes never left the offending visitor, he never glanced at her, but looked everywhere

"LOOK OUT—I THINK HE'S GOING TO PULL A KNIFE!"

THE OFFENDING VISITOR

else, humming to himself, just sitting. Slowly, slowly, eyes always on the squatter, Moddom crept her way up to the fence, stopped, and later moved from fence to trellis, while the other cat said to himself, "Delightful weather we're having. A nice day. A charming vista." Finally, Moddom reached the top of the arbor, eyes on the cat, still crouching, body taut—and after an eternally long pause, she moved a step closer. They were now separated by several feet. I watched motionless—fearful that the slightest noise or movement might spoil the climax of this drama. The other cat hummed a little tune, still paying no apparent notice. Moddom, still eyeing the cat, moved another step closer, hunched down, and then another step, even closer. Without ever looking at her, the other cat said, "A lovely day, a pleasant visit. I think I'll see how things are going next door," and stepped lightly to the fence and down into the other yard.

I felt as if I had been witnessing a potential military engagement. Like an old battleship moving deliberately and readying its guns against a visible challenge, Moddom had maintained her sovereignty without firing a shot. She returned to the yard, which was unmistakably hers, and on subsequent days she continued dropping in at the apartment.

I got Bella a box of toys, which included a little ball with a tinkling bell in it. This fascinated her less than the opened box, the paper and the string, which were real fun. And then there were the catnip mice. They came in different colors and I got several.

Bella showed a modest interest in them, and played with them a little. Whatever catnip did for adult cats, it apparently didn't do for this kitten. But the effect on Moddom was spectacular. She grabbed a catnip mouse and tore off its cloth covering. Then on to the rest of them. She practically inhaled the catnip. She couldn't get enough of it. She rolled on the floor. She pranced. She danced. She laughed. She sang. She leaped in the air, she did handsprings. She was absolutely plastered. Bella watched all these antics, turning her head this way and that, moving her little paws back to give Momma room for her gymnastics and taking it all in with her most OH expression.

Came the dawn. When Moddom finally sobered up, she hated herself and she hated me. She saw her performance as a version of Noah's drunkenness, and regarded me as the agent of her undoing. I had brought this catnip stuff into the house. I had let her make a fool of herself in front of her young daughter. When she left, talking to herself and probably nursing a hangover, I wasn't sure if she'd come back.

Bella moved on toward larger kittenhood and cathood. With only a little instruction from Moddom, she learned how to claw up the furniture and curtains and how to ignore the store-bought scratching post I got for her. She also found the specially designed and upholstered basket I gave her less to her liking than sleeping on chairs, on my bed or other places. From the way she slept in new different locations you would suppose Moddom had told her some catnapper or hit man might be after her.

SHE PRANCED. SHE DANCED.

She soon picked up all the household cat tricks. She knew how to get in the way of my feet when I was in a hurry—and, when I was in bed, how to pounce on my stomach. She later learned how to put her head down to "make a neck" when she wanted to be scratched—"a little farther up...closer to the ear... more to the left...that's it..." And she turned on her purr machine when I performed satisfactorily.

At other times she could be cool and distant. I think Moddom's early teachings must have included, "Just because he buys you dinner doesn't mean he can paw you."

As Bella grew a bit bigger, she took over and became mistress of the house, sometimes making little

I WASN'T SURE IF SHE'D COME BACK

18

comments when the service was less than adequate.

She discovered how to tell time, guess the outside temperature and decide to go out late on cold nights. This naturally included the endless hesitant stand in the open doorway until my feet nearly froze, and I would yell, "For God's sake, Bella—*In* or *Out*!" At which she would remind me with a withering look that I was the doorman, and that she would decide in or out when she pleased. Then, after staying out just long enough for me to return to bed, she would make enough racket to wake the neighborhood as she demanded back in and asked what was the delay. When I grumbled about this, she would say, "If you'd give me my own key, I wouldn't have to wait for you" and "with a little change in a pair of mittens, I wouldn't have to bother you about food either. If I'm so much trouble, just let me know. I can take care of myself. I can get a room."

Sometimes I would get back to sleep still hearing her muttering, "There are places where I'm *wanted*— there are people who'd *appreciate* me"—on and on into the night.

Bella had no complaint about bathroom facilities. She had the back yard, where Moddom had explained to her the advantage of constantly reminding people that cats are neater than dogs; and indoors she had taken to the sandbox easily. It was interesting to see how Bella, in the box, assumed the same air of vacant intensity that everyone does in that situation. I once got down on all fours and tried to look her in the eye while she was sitting in the box. She turned away from me and let me know that she found this intrusion into her privacy in appalling bad taste, which I guess it was. "Maybe you'd like to give me a magazine to read," she muttered. But I was just curious about whether I could get her attention at such a time.

Bella was constantly washing herself and preening. She would lick lick lick, wash wash wash. More than that—in the sandbox she would keep covering the most piddling effort over and over again with incessant pawing and scratching until she nearly wore a hole in the box. I'd finally yell, "Bella! For Chri-sake, Enough!"

And as she continued kicking the sand back vigorously enough to send it spraying out of the box and onto the carpet and a nearby bookshelf, she would keep saying, "Neat. I'm neat. We cats are *Neat. Neat, NEAT!*" She didn't say in so many words that some people are not so neat, although I was aware that I had lots of old newspapers and magazines and clothes scattered around, and that my apartment didn't look like something out of *House and Garden*. More directly, I got the message that she wanted the sand changed more frequently. I fully expected her to come in some day carrying a sign saying, "NEATNESS COUNTS." You have no idea how distracting it can be to hear a cat constantly tossing sand around and saying, "Neat, Neat, *Neat!*"

Once when she saw me watching her interminable toilette with much paw licking, she stopped momentarily, looked back at me and said, "The paws that refreshes." I don't know where she picked this up— probably from television. But I paid no attention. If I had said anything, it would only have encouraged her— like the time I observed that she was a bona fide cat, and she said, "fishbona fide." I told her that one needed more work. It wasn't just the things she said—it was the way she smirked when she said them.

Being in service to Bella naturally meant being doorman and chef as well as waiter. But she didn't require me to wear a gold-braided uniform or a chef's hat. Nothing showy. Just prompt attendance. As a person given to late snacks, I would sometimes make my way quietly to the kitchen at night. Bella, even though sound asleep, seemed to have some kind of built-in antenna or super-hearing, which could detect the almost noiseless opening of the refrigerator door as if it were beaming an alarm. She would come into the kitchen with her eyes still closed to ask, "What have we got here? What's for tonight?"

At regular mealtimes when she found the service not fast enough, she would run around, leading me to the kitchen, and mumbling, "Here it is. For God's sake, he can't even find the fridge without my help. Over here—put the dish down *here*! Sometimes I wonder how he manages to dress himself in the morning—can hardly find the kitchen, forgodsake."

While I was preparing her dinner, she would run around between my legs and even climb up on the table. I would have to put her down to avoid the risk of her tail getting in the way when I was chopping up kidneys or liver for her.

But no matter how hungry she was or how appetizing the meal, she always kept me in my place. She might run back and forth like crazy while I was preparing the food and serving it, as if she could not wait to have it placed before her. But when I set it down, she never began eating without putting her nose to the dish first—and then, arching an eyebrow, looking up to say, "This you call food? This is dining? This is gracious living?" Not till after that preliminary show of disdain would she dig in.

That was when dinner was its best.

When it was NOT particularly to her liking, she would look at it, detect the slightest bit of crust, touch

I HATED IT WHEN SHE DID THAT

her paw to it, give me a look of disgust and walk around it. "Hardly fresh," she would mutter. "Less than tasty."

The only time she expressed total contempt for what I had served, she did it without saying a thing. She looked at the dish, sniffed, looked at me, and then turned her back to the dish and began digging at the carpet with her hind feet as if covering something in her sandbox. Then she stalked off. She didn't have to say anything. Whatever it was, I never served it again.

What really used to get me, though, was something she would do at times when she had just finished a hearty repast. After a little stretching, yawning and general relaxing, she would inform me that she was ready to go out and that I might now do my doorman service. What she would do then, when she got out, was to pull in her stomach, suck in her cheeks and look undernourished and forlorn as she slumped her way down the porch past the neighbors' doors. "Poor dear," they would say as they observed this Little-Match-Girl act, and serve up some whipping cream or other delicacy for her. I never heard her actually say, "He doesn't feed me." But with that starving-refugee number she put on, it wasn't necessary. I hated it when she did that.

Unfortunately, my work and my social schedule didn't always fit into Bella's schedule. And when I came home late, she tapped her foot, paced around and really laid on the guilt. "Oh, you've finally decided to come home," she would say. "And of course you've had dinner. Oh yes, it doesn't make any difference that *I*

"WELL, YOU'VE FINALLY DECIDED TO COME HOME"

haven't had dinner. That's perfectly all right. No need to concern yourself about *me*. My, you seem to have dined very well (sniffing)—steak and mushrooms, I believe (sniff) perhaps a touch of béarnaise sauce. Very good. Very good. Don't worry about me at all—hungry and sitting here by myself. No need for anyone to worry about *me*. I just *live* here." All this would go on while I was preparing her dinner. In a way, I think she almost enjoyed my tardiness. She probably spent her time thinking up comments and little sarcasms.

I was used to Bella giving me a hard time when I came in late. But going away for a weekend presented real problems. Leaving a lot of food out would have resulted in her sulking and touching nothing after the first fresh meal. There are probably devices with built-in timers that deliver food on schedule. But I doubt that Bella would have cared for what one of these things dished out. And despite all her talk about how she could take care of herself, I knew she wanted to be waited on. A friend in another apartment agreed to cat-sit, and even to take Bella in for a few days.

The trip to the apartment upstairs awakened Bella's fears about What Is He Up To? and Where Are We Going?

When we arrived at the apartment and I explained that she would be staying here a couple of days or so, she began examining her surroundings, sniffing every inch of floorboard and furniture. Satisfied that she had cased it for booby-traps and was familiar with terrain, she decided that she would somehow put up with it and survive.

A few days later, when I returned to pick her up, she hid under the bed. "Who is he?" she asked, "What does he want?" She knew damn well who I was and what I wanted. I had come to take her back home, but she had to go through this routine of letting me know that I had abandoned her and was just someone that she used to know.

Bella had long since put kittenhood behind her and—far from popping up in file drawers—she had taken to spending her time atop shelves and bookcases and threading her way through the bric-a-brac on the mantel. As she grew into cathood, she took to lying about, posturing and saying, "Look, I'm adorable."

"WHO IS HE? WHAT DOES HE WANT?"

28

"LOOK, I'M ADORABLE"

If she could have found lipstick, rouge and powder, she probably would have used them. I told her this was revolting, but it didn't have any effect on her. When I told her to knock it off on the "adorable" stuff, she said, "I'm a full-blooded cat." This was something she heard me say when visitors asked about her. I never knew when she would pick up some casual comment like that and play it back.

I used to think she might be turning on the TV, smoking my cigarettes and drinking my wine while I was at the office. But I didn't really know. I also wondered about some of the calls on my phone bills but never mentioned any of these things to her.

One day Bella took me to the door, and I opened it to see several other cats. When they saw me they ran various distances—some making rapid time down the porch—others going only a few feet. They all waited. They looked at me and they looked at the one they had come to call on—Bella.

Bella looked back at them. These gentlemen cats— and I use the term broadly—came in a variety of sizes, styles and colors—solids, stripes and mixed patterns. They were black, brown, gray, orange, calico, with combinations of markings. A few seemed fairly kempt with reasonably good coats, while others looked pretty scruffy. They all waited while Bella calmly sized them up. After a long time, she turned back into the house and signaled to me that I might close the door now. I didn't know whether she was reluctant to leave maid- enhood, whether she felt there was not an attractive one in the bunch, whether she decided to keep them guessing, or simply wasn't in the mood. And of course she didn't say.

The suitors kept returning and standing around on the porch. And whenever I opened the door, they scattered and stopped, as in a game where children "freeze" in different positions. They followed this usual procedure when Bella let me know that she was ready to see her admirers again—or rather to let them see her. At her appearance, some of them later approached cautiously and made little advances, which Bella turned aside.

In time, she allowed one of the bolder cats to come nearer, and they literally began going around together, the suitor getting closer to Bella, his head behind hers and his body alongside, while they made little circles together. Finally he took her neck in his mouth as they continued around in a kind of ritual dance.

The moment his mouth closed on her neck the other cats knew it was all over. She was his, just as certainly as if she and her suitor had exchanged vows and rings and taken off on a honeymoon express. A couple of the other cats said, as they turned to trot off, "I hear there are some pretty good mice around here." Another said, "Holy smoke, I didn't realize what time it was—I have an important engagement." And one of the more raffish ones, trying to save face, gave a weak little smile and said, "I was just out for a stroll." Making their excuses, they all left; and eventually Bella and her fiancé went on their way together. I left a light on for her.

GENTLEMEN CALLERS

A night or two later, I heard Bella at the door demanding to be let in. She went by me at a brisk pace with an "I've-been-on-important-business" expression on her face, saying as she passed, "Dinner!" A cat who had achieved full felinehood and worldliness, she didn't feel like engaging in small talk. She had dinner and promptly went to sleep—out cold.

"DINNER!"

Neither of us said anything about her personal life. Her comings and goings were none of my business, and she knew that I would remain in service as doorman, chef and butler.

Bella did not make a big deal out of her pregnancy; in fact, she didn't show it. But eventually the time came when she got inside a partly open closet in my bedroom, and took to stomping down an old shirt, some beat-up trousers, a pair of sneakers, assorted socks and whatever else was lying at the bottom, to prepare a proper place for her accouchement.

And one morning I discovered that The Event had taken place. There was Bella with a tiny newborn solid black kitten. Not a litter—just one. I didn't know whether she decided to do it just like people or whether she thought she'd just try one for size, but that was it.

Of course, I waited on Bella hand and paw, making sure she had whatever she wanted to eat, and ready with warm milk if she wanted any for her offspring. And off I went to work.

Then came The Mysterious Disappearance.

Bella was up and about, but no kitten was to be seen. I looked all over the apartment but no kitten. When I asked Bella, she looked puzzled. "Kitten? Kitten? What do you mean?"

This was not just a one-day mystery. I continued to look everywhere, while Bella went about the house apparently unconcerned—whistling and humming to herself, buffing her nails and acting as if I must be suffering some kind of delusion.

I inquired of friends and neighbors, who had no

clues but offered dark stories they had heard of even the nicest animals devouring their young. The thought of cat cannibalism was too horrible to accept. Nevertheless, I examined the nest closely for any clues, fur or foul. There were none. Bella acted as if I must really be out of my mind. Whatever was I looking for? "Come on, Bella, dammit, I didn't just imagine this." She let on that she didn't know what on earth I was talking about.

But one evening I heard a small "meow." It took awhile to determine the exact location, but there it was in a narrow space between the back of a bookcase and the wall. I tried to wedge in a hand to lift it out, but now that the game was up, Bella retrieved it by herself. She didn't say, "Oh, THAT kitten," and she didn't apologize or explain. She just licked the little black furry thing and looked at me.

The Moddom had obviously taught Bella, right at the beginning, "Trust no one—especially that guy who feeds you." For all I know, the Moddom might even have taken Bella aside and said, "Listen—guys don't like dames with kids. You have a kid and he'll sell you both right down the river." Of course, in all fairness, I don't know that Moddom ever told her that.

Anyhow —

I fussed over Bella and her kitten and explained that I was happy for both of them.

With the cat out of the bag, so to speak, Bella now gave full attention to motherhood, and watched while I put out warm milk for Baby Bella. It didn't have a name yet, but before long became so active that I decided to call it Hazel, after a current hurricane of the same name.

You might not think so, but it's hard to tell about kittens when they are very small. At least so I was told by friends who assured me that I had not flunked Feline Biology 101 when Hazel later turned out to be a boy. I changed the name to Hazy and he answered just as well.

Now Bella was the little madonna, lying in the same chair the Moddom had occupied, languidly switching her tail while Hazy leaped in the air making passes at it.

Hazy was friendly, boisterous, and adventurous, a little ball of energy. He slid and scooted across table tops. He invited me to play with him. I think he'd have fetched my slippers if I had wanted him to, but I'd never have asked him to do anything so uncatly. When he was big enough to go in the back yard, that was a real frolic.

It was Hazy, of course, who had to climb the lone tree in that yard—and having climbed it, he simply stayed there. I pleaded with him to come down, but with no success. I put out fish and a bowl of cream for him but he remained aloft. Neighbors in the building saw all this and began to come out. Soon quite a group had gathered, several with suggestions that didn't work out. Finally, one of them decided to call the fire department. A fire truck dispatched on a cat-in-tree mission was just the kind of a big to-do I had hoped to avoid. But I couldn't leave little Hazy up there indefinitely.

The firemen went about their business of hauling in a ladder that could be extended to the proper height.

HAZY

They patiently maneuvered it through narrow hallways, around steps to yard, and carefully coped with tree branches until they were able to set it up properly. Hazy sat and watched all this with great interest. Then, after a fireman had mounted the ladder and got halfway up, Hazy smiled and—ignoring fireman and ladder—scampered down the tree by himself. He loved every moment of it.

Bella later had a two-kitten litter and Hazy acted like a proud uncle or big brother, happy to play with the smaller ones.

Now when I went to the fridge late at night, I was soon heading a little parade, with Bella up front, followed by Hazy, followed by new kittens—all of them half asleep but marching to the kitchen.

A LITTLE PARADE

I thought I'd keep the kittens, and did for a while. But as Bella got into production, it was obvious that I couldn't keep all her progeny or even one from each little batch. I was determined not to have any kittens done in, and neither Bella nor I wanted a vet to do a job on her. So I began passing out kittens. A kitten in the hand is worth several in an ad. When it comes to selling jobs, these wide-eyed innocents make the craftiest salesmen look like dolts. Since there were always takers, I didn't have to descend to the last-ditch device of visiting friends with young children and pulling kittens out of my pockets for the kids to play with. I don't know if I'd ever have resorted to that. But I was glad I wasn't put to the test.

Being a kitten dispenser kept the population down, but it didn't do anything for domestic tranquility. As kittens disappeared, Bella and Hazy took to looking all over the apartment for them—ironically, just as I had searched for Bella's first born—and asking, "Where are they? Where ARE they?" The first time was the hardest. I tried to distract Bella and Hazy. I tried to play with them; I prepared special dishes for them, but it was no use. Hazy summarized it all when I was down on the floor trying to make up to him. He kept turning his head away from me. When I asked what was the matter, he looked away, lowered his head and murmured, "You know what you did." I knew, and I felt awful about it. It took time before they would forget—especially Hazy. Bella had said something under her breath to the effect that her mother had warned her about this. But as time went on, I guess she figured she could always have more kittens—and did.

Time heals. Hazy was soon his old self again, waking me in the morning by putting his nose to mine, wanting to play and bounding around full of beans. But tragedy was in the offing.

Hazy took sick. At first I thought he was just a little off his feed, or that he needed to cough up a fur ball, the kind of thing I had gone through with Bella. But Bella got to worrying too. "He's really sick," she said. I bundled him up and took him to a local vet establishment, where they assured me they would have him back in shape in no time. Hazy called to me as I left. He had never been in such strange and noisy surroundings and must have thought he had been forsaken. Each day I phoned this place, and each time they assured me that Hazy was coming along fine and they needed just another day before he'd be ready to go home with me. After several days, I insisted on seeing him and said that I was coming over that afternoon. Shortly afterward they called back to say that unfortunately he had just died. I thought they were quacks and later when I found that this "pet hospital" was no longer there, I hoped they had gone out of business permanently. What I actually hoped was that they would fry in hell permanently.

Moddom was seen less and less frequently. I think she felt she had done everything she could for Bella, who had reached full cathood. And as Moddom continued her ratting and dating, she may not have wanted her latest tomcat friends to know she was a grandmother. If Bella missed her, she never said anything about it.

Cats either have a lot of resilience or lousy memories. For Bella, life went on. She had been around long enough to see the world and to become, in her own more restrained way, supervisor of the domain once ruled by Moddom. I never saw her in an actual fight, but I heard fighting going on, and I saw Bella trot in the door with just enough fur missing to indicate that she'd been in a tussle. More to the point, I never saw other cats encroach on her territory and knew that she upheld the family tradition and dominion over the yard. The only callers were her gentlemen friends, and she handled them with aplomb.

Bella also had her moments indoors. A television show that conducted long-distance interviews with people sent out a camera crew to set up equipment in the apartment. The program began with a short tour of my cluttered quarters, after which I sat next to a table for the conversation with the TV host, who was in another city. In the middle of the program, Bella jumped up on the table, paraded back and forth, stepping and turning like a model on a runway. She smiled at the camera, bowed, and did a few queen-mother waves to the viewing audience. She really hammed it up.

The producers never had a subject quite like her. She was a star. I heard afterward from many people who saw what they regarded as The Bella Show and sent her their compliments. I think some of them wanted her paw prints.

Bella took it all in stride and everything returned to normal in the apartment and the yard. But eventually both would be scheduled to go.

One day came a notice that the entire building was to be torn down and all tenants—including Bella and me—had to vacate in a matter of weeks. To make matters worse, an illness put me into a hospital for an extended stay. Friends looked after Bella and even found me a new apartment—but in a building where cats were not allowed. It was only later that I learned the manager had a cat herself, and I supposed Bella could have been smuggled into the new quarters. But in this high-rise without the yard and without her nights on the town, it wouldn't have been the same.

Meanwhile, in my absence an acquaintance was found who wanted a cat, had a suitable place and was glad to provide a home for Bella.

It was a matter of several weeks before I was able to visit and to give Bella the reassurance I felt she needed that I was still around and cared for her.

When I arrived at the apartment, Bella was brought out from another room for the happy surprise. She looked uncomfortable and said nothing. After having a drink with the hostess, I got down on the floor with Bella, who was facing the other side of the room. I told her that here I was and I had come to see her in her new surroundings. She was silent for a moment; then — still looking away — she said, out of the side of her mouth, "I've got it good here. Make believe you don't know me."

I kept glancing at Bella from time to time during some more conversation with the woman who now shared living quarters with her, and prepared to leave.

Bella's back was to us as she sat looking into the glowing fireplace. This time I was the one standing in a doorway and hesitating. "I'm going now," I said in a loud voice—and waited.

"Goodbye Bella," I called.

She never even turned around.